be a parent not a pal

Dr Jeff Kemp

First published in 2010
Australian Academic Press
32 Jeays Street
Bowen Hills Qld 4006
Australia
www.australianacademicpress.com.au

Copyright © 2010 text Jeff Kemp.
Copyright © 2010 cartoons Australian Academic Press Pty Ltd.

Copying for educational purposes
The *Australian Copyright Act 1968* (Cwlth) allows a maximum of one chapter or 10% of this book, whichever is the greater, to be reproduced and/or communicated by any educational institution for its educational purposes provided that the educational institution (or the body that administers it) has given a remuneration notice to Copyright Agency Limited (CAL) under the Act.
For details of the CAL licence for educational institutions contact:
Copyright Agency Limited, 19/157 Liverpool Street, Sydney, NSW 2000.
E-mail info@copyright.com.au

Production and communication for other purposes
Except as permitted under the Act, for example a fair dealing for the purposes of study, research, criticism or review, no part of this book may be reproduced, stored in a retrieval system, or transmitted in any form or by any means electronic, mechanical, photocopying, recording or otherwise without prior written permission of the copyright holder.

National Library of Australia Cataloguing-in-Publication entry:

Author:	Kemp, Jeff.
Title:	Be a parent not a pal / Jeff Kemp.
ISBN:	9781921513480 (pbk.)
Subjects:	Parenting.
	Parent and teenager.
Dewey Number:	649.125

Cartoons by Matt Mawson. Cover designed by Maria Biaggini.
Typeset in Sabon 12pt by Australian Academic Press.

"A wonderfully practical roadmap for parents journeying through the teenage years. Simple but effective common-sense parenting guidelines presented in a conversational style by a genuine, caring, down-to-earth parent, educator and counsellor."

Mary Wallis
Previous Principal of two Catholic Schools
Presently Area Supervisor, Brisbane Catholic Education

"As parents of a troubled and difficult teenager, we understand how hard parenting can be. Struggling to maintain a positive relationship with our son, we felt isolated clueless and full of self-doubt. For the past few years we have been 'running on empty'. But, in all this we have been truly blessed with the support and guidance of Dr Jeff Kemp, the guidance counsellor at our son's school.

The 'Asteros' program, founded by Dr Kemp, supports troubled teenagers who are underachieving to develop self-awareness and commit to bettering their lives. Our son has benefited greatly from this program. Dr Kemp's parenting program has helped us better understand how our son is 'wired' from a behavioural perspective. It has reaffirmed our faith in making reasonable parenting decisions without being worried about how they might affect our relationship with our son. Above all, Dr Kemp has helped us believe and actually feel that although our son was created by us, he was not us.

We continue to negotiate our way through these troubling times, but it is with some degree of inner peace amidst the turmoil. It is impossible to convey in words how grateful we are for Dr Kemp's support and compassion on our journey so far. He has been an absolute rock for our entire family."

Sherrie and Peter Davis
Worongary, Queensland, Australia

"At last! A guide that treats parents with respect and offers real comfort and support in the often baffling world of child rearing. Dr Kemp has honed his skills by not only successfully raising his own children but also by working with challenging children and teens in school and community settings. He has brought his practical experience as a father and his professional perspectives together to create a unique collection of reading and reflections. These are a representative sample of case studies that will quickly lead parents to more informed and careful decision making about their children are also featured.

I highly recommend this book to parents and other professionals whose daily lives will be shaped and strengthened by better understanding themselves as well as their children and teens. Have not enjoyed a parenting book as much since Coloroso's 'Kids are worth it'!"

Dr Loretta Giorcelli, OAM FACE
Professor of Special Education and Child Development
Sydney, Australia

Foreword

More than ever, parents are struggling with parenting troubled and disengaged teenagers. Parenting a teenager has never been easy, but so many added pressures and circumstances that weren't in existence twenty or thirty years ago now impact greatly on this most important of roles.

Parents at times feel so alone in this difficult journey and seek support from wherever they can find it. Dr Jeff Kemp is an academic, educator, counsellor and, most importantly, a dedicated parent of four adult children who has been providing this wonderful support in a variety of ways to parents, teenagers and families for over thirty years. His advice is based on practical and sometimes homespun wisdom and experience, which comes as a result of walking with and sharing in a variety of family journeys. His compassion and enthusiasm has helped the most troubled of students re-engage with their family, society and school. Many success stories of teenagers who were written off by schools and society have been attributed to the patient, wise and, when needed, firm guidance of Jeff Kemp.

In recent years, Jeff has developed the Asteros program to provide early intervention for 'at risk' teenagers. A unique aspect of this program has been the Wilderness component, where young, at-risk adolescents are taken out of their comfort zone and challenged and supported to change directions in their troubled lives. For many this experience has been life changing and life giving. One of the vital components of all the counselling work undertaken by Jeff is the establishment of powerful and positive partnerships with parents and families — no matter how diverse and fractured some of these may be. This is the essence of the success that his program has enjoyed.

It has been my privilege over many years to have worked closely with Jeff Kemp and know how grateful parents have been for the informative, enjoyable and practical parenting programs he has prepared and presented. What is presented here is an easy-to-read, relevant summary of much of what has been discussed and shared in these programs.

We all love our children dearly, no one more so than Jeff and myself. However, as the title suggests, in the teenage years we are fully aware it was not always possible to be their pal if good and effective parenting was to be achieved. The wonderful benefit of being a parent, not a pal to your teenager, is that in the adult years, in many cases, your children do become your best friends. Who could ask for more than that?

Happy reading and parenting.

Mary Wallis
Previous Principal of two Catholic Schools
Presently Area Supervisor, Brisbane Catholic Education

Contents

Foreword v
Acknowledgments...ix
About the author xi

Chapter 1
A few words to begin 1

Chapter 2
Thoughts on parenting
a teenager 7

Chapter 3
Being a teenager....................................19

Chapter 4
Parenting with purpose
and patience 29

Chapter 5
Teen topics 47
Friends 48
Body image 51
Depression 53
Self-harm 55
Suicide..57
Sexuality..58
Drugs and alcohol 60
Technology 63

Chapter 6

Teen scenarios … 65

Broken-hearted … 67
Bush lawyer … 69
'Big T' … 72
Coming out … 74
Cyber bully … 76
Dark thoughts … 78
Fair-weather friend … 80
Family ties … 82
Greener grass … 84
Hidden gift … 87
Hot breakfast … 89
Hung up … 91
Hurt … 92
Money matters … 94
On the edge … 95
Off the rails … 98
Runaway … 100
Scratcher … 102
Spellbound … 104
Self-exile … 106
Newcomer … 108
Over-indulged … 110
Independence … 112
Real friend … 114
Schemer … 116

Chapter 7

In conclusion … 117

Acknowledgments

Many people have inspired and encouraged me in writing this book. I am particularly grateful to Terry Hannagan for his wisdom, wicked sense of humour, and magnificent outlook on life.

I am humbled and sincerely thankful for the positive feedback on my work from the many parents who have completed my *Be a Parent Not a Pal* parent skilling program. I am particularly grateful to the parents of troubled youth who have participated in my *Asteros* program for reminding me time and again of the wondrous abiding love, although sometimes tested, of a parent for their child.

Special thanks go to my publisher Stephen May for his meticulous editorial support and to Amanda for her enthusiasm and flair.

Finally I wish to thank my wife Deborah and children Mattese, Serne, Denan and Keshnee for their support during my self imposed exile to write this book.

About the author

A father of four, Jeff is a highly successful educator with over 30 years experience as a primary school teacher, a secondary school teacher, a university lecturer, a presenter at National and State conferences and a specialist guidance counsellor of children and teenagers, in particular troubled teenagers. In addition to his Doctorate of Education, he holds bachelor degrees in both arts and education, and graduate diplomas in educational psychology, special education, and leadership studies. He is currently head of student support services at St Michael's College, Merrimac, on Queensland's Gold Coast.

Jeff's highly successful early intervention program for troubled 'at-risk' teenagers, 'Asteros', involves a range of interventions, including a wilderness adventure experience, intensive in-school student support, parent training and ongoing support from a volunteer mentor or life coach. The program was awarded a recognition bursary from Griffith University, which enabled Jeff to visit and study the very best programs for troubled teenagers in the United States. Jeff has since incorporated the research findings into his current practice. He also provides an online individual support service for parents of children and teenagers.

For 15 years Jeff has been president of a community Sports Club and co-founded an annual international youth football tournament which has grown in 12 years to be the largest of its kind in the southern hemisphere.

Jeff's work has been recognised in State and Commonwealth Government awards for his outstanding contribution to youth in the community. For more information on the Asteros program and other support materials for parents and youth go to: www.parentingtodaysteenager.com.au.

Chapter

1

A few words to begin …

At first glance the title of this book 'Be a Parent Not a Pal' might seem a bit odd. Why would a caring parent not want to be their teenager's pal — their best friend, the one they turn to for help? Well, you can provide this role for your child but it has to be something created out of the first vital role you must play — a parent.

In recent years I have noted two alarming trends that are straining the role of parenting today. One is the increasing number of teenagers who operate on the mistaken belief that the world revolves around them — that they have entitlement and as such their every wish should be met in an instant. As a consequence many parents feel they are under constant siege. Their authority is often questioned with statements such as: 'You can't do that. I know my rights'. Typically, parents believe that unless they meet their teenager's every demand their teenager will stop loving them. As the demands and pressures continue, the parents begin to feel disempowered and helpless and may be tempted to 'give up' on parenting. The other trend is a significant increase in the number of teenagers who progressively disengage from school and eventually drop out before graduation. Many of these teenagers live in a troubled family, display severe challenging behaviour, have a learning disability, or misuse substances. They experience great difficulty accessing the school curriculum and are at high risk of not completing the compulsory years of schooling. The unfortunate predictable outcome for many of these teenagers is long-term unemployment, mental health difficulties, and involvement with the juvenile justice system. No wonder that the parents of these teenagers are frequently at the point of despair and at a total loss on how to continue to parent their teenager.

Concerned with these trends I used my many years of experience working with parents and teenagers — in particular, troubled teenagers — to devise an approach that would help parents prevent such a parenting breakdown. The basis of this approach is the observation that when a parent has a plan and follows that plan to allow for parenting with a purpose, they in fact can become their teenager's pal.

Teaching and encouraging parents how to formulate a plan and follow it produced the 'Parent Not a Pal' program for parents of teenagers enrolled in schools in

A few words to begin ...

my local community. At the same time I also commenced the 'Asteros' program for troubled teenagers enrolled in schools in the wider region. ('Asteros' is an ancient Greek word meaning bright star.) I firmly believe that every teenager has a unique gift that should be identified and nurtured along with community-valued personal qualities, including responsibility, commitment, dependability, loyalty, humility, honesty and sense of humour. If a teenager develops and maintains a real sense of self-worth and displays community-valued personal qualities the chances of them achieving their full potential is greatly enhanced.

The Asteros program runs for 12 months and involves the establishment and maintenance of close working partnerships with organisations and groups in the community, including the troubled teenager's school, outdoor educators from the Police Citizens Youth Club, and select interest groups and sporting associations. It includes a two-part wilderness adventure/therapy experience, the Parent not a Pal training program for parents, regular in-school learning support and personal counselling, outside school support from government youth mental services if required, and ongoing support from a trained volunteer mentor/life coach. The program has achieved outstanding success to date, with 80 per cent of the first group of program participants completing their schooling. Further ongoing research is now informing updates to the program and its success was recognised by Griffith University through a special bursary that enabled me to travel to the United States to study their own wilderness adventure therapy-based programs for troubled teenagers.

What I have learned from all of this, is that there are many parents out there who need a little quality straight-forward advice and a dose of inspiration and caring to give them the skills and confidence to effectively parent their teenager on their journey through the teenage years to adulthood — especially those teenagers who are on what I think of as being a 'developmental' holiday.

In the pages that follow I have tried to convey some of the messages that have been so successful in helping the many parents and teenagers whom I have had the honour of working with over many years. It is not a list of steps, rules, or laws to follow, but rather a sincere expression of what really matters in the journey of parenting — the sorts of personal things we think in our private moments about what it means to be a parent, and the hopes we have for our children. To lighten the load a little and provoke some thought along this journey, I have sprinkled throughout the first five chapters various 'Wise Owl' quotations and humorous truisms I think are relevant to the topic, as well as a series of 'Road Signs' to help remind you of some of the more important issues along the journey you and your teenager are making.

The final section of the book covers common teen topics and what every parent should know about them, and 25 scenarios in which you as a parent can place yourself to explore and practise planned parenting, in a wide variety of circumstances.

The advice is practical at times, and emotionally important at others. It comes from my life experiences, my university studies, psychological research, and the ongoing learning opportunities I am constantly finding in my professional career.

I hope you find it useful.

Chapter

2

Thoughts on parenting a teenager

"If you look deeply into the palm of your hand, you will see your parents and all generations of their ancestors. All of them alive in this moment. Each is present in your body. You are a continuation of each of these people."
— Thich Nhat Hanh

Being a parent is one of the very few vocations in life that doesn't require formal education, training, apprenticeship, or a professional license to practice. There is no prescribed 'how to' manual with answers for every parenting challenge you will face. But because there is no such thing as a parent licence there is also no such thing as a perfect parent. Just like your teenager you are a real person with strengths and limitations.

Without doubt, parenting a teenager is a tough challenge. It takes purpose, creativity, determination and patience. While it has always been a challenge, parenting a teenager in today's fast-changing complex world presents a far greater challenge than it was for your parents and the generations before.

In past times your parents and their parents had, for the most part, a fairly reliable parenting template set out for them to follow. The world did not change greatly from one generation to the next, families were less mobile, and parents had a strong support system of not only successful parenting examples to follow, but also helping hands from nearby living relations and close friends.

Today you are parenting in a far different world — a world in which the only certainty is change. Yesteryear parenting templates are simply not suitable to equip a teenager with the skills and confidence needed to achieve their potential in today's ever-changing world.

The pace of modern life can sometimes make any parent feel they are in danger of losing control of their children as they outpace you with their internet-gained knowledge, worldly cynicism and mature posturing. But you must not forget that your role in their lives is to be their parent and that without this role they will lose a vital component of their upbringing. No matter how hard you might try to keep up with the pace of their lives, you will ultimately fail if you try to communicate with them as their friends do. Your teenager sees you as their parent.

Thoughts on parenting a teenager

 "We shall not cease from exploration, but the end of our exploring will be to return to the same place, and know it for the first time."
— T.S. Elliot

However, in following your parenting role, you need not abandon elements of friendly communication and sharing that stem from the everyday relationship you have with your teenager. You are each living parts of your lives closely with each other and it is entirely appropriate to share a laugh, an animated conversation, an exchange of gossip along the way. Your serious role as a parent need not always be the dominating factor in your home life, nor require an always stern and authoritative approach. Polite, respectful, friendly conversation is a healthy way for both parents and teenagers to communicate with each other.

How you parent your teenager will be very much determined by two major influences. One influence is the memory you have of the way you were brought up and the other is the influence on you of others in your 'life-world'. Your life-world includes your family, your work colleagues, your friends and the media.

Irrespective of the mix of past and present influences that shape your particular belief and way of parenting, to be effective you need to see parenting as a way of life, not just as a job. You need to be a full-time parent to ensure your teenager has the skills and confidence needed to achieve their potential and lead a full and meaningful life in today's increasingly complex world.

Parenting a teenager requires energy and sustained effort over an extended period of time. You need to maintain purpose, confidence and patience to face the challenges that lie ahead of you. Remember, parenting a teenager is not a sprint, it is a marathon run. You need to be in it for the long haul.

The parenting challenge you will face as you journey with your teenager through the teenage years will not be unlike taking a roller-coaster ride. For most of us such a ride is one we face with a touch of anxiety and fear. We expect it to be a wild ride travelling at breakneck speed, with lots of unpredictable fast-changing twists and turns. However, we also know that many riders before us have taken the ride and survived. We too expect to survive and to remember the exhilarating experience with a sense of accomplishment.

So it is with parenting a teenager. Most new parents are apprehensive about parenting during the 'terrible teen' years. They have all heard about the things that can and do go wrong. However, just like roller-coaster riders, they also know that many parents before them have survived — even enjoyed — parenting through the teenager years, and have gone on to have a positive mature relationship with their teenager as an adult.

You should think of parenting your teenager as a journey of self-discovery for yourself and a journey of

Thoughts on parenting a teenager

self-discovery for your teenager. Ideally before starting the journey you need to take time to really get to know yourself — 'the real you, warts and all' — and accept yourself as the unique person you are, and commit yourself fully to parenting your teenager.

During the journey your teenager also needs to get to know themselves, accept themselves as the unique person they are, and commit themselves to be the very best they can be in their life. This means developing self-understanding, self-acceptance and self-commitment. But that doesn't happen overnight. It takes time, persistence and patience. What is important is that you are both willing to take the journey.

 "I dream my parenting then paint my picture."
— Vincent Van Gogh

To maximise your parenting effectiveness you need to have a 'Parent Wish' to guide your thinking and action as you go about the day-to-day parenting of your teenager. Your Parent Wish represents the inner most enduring wish you hold for your teenager in life.

You may not necessarily be consciously aware of it, but you probably already have a goal for your children (a wish) that guides the way you parent your teenager. Typically, this might be for your teenager to develop into a happy, healthy, well-adjusted adult capable of facing life's challenges and living a full and meaningful life. That's your Parent Wish at its simplest.

The Parent Wish I have for my own teenager is that on their journey through life they grow in self-knowledge, self-acceptance and self-commitment and that they have the personality that will help them go well in life, including a sense of responsibility, respect for others, honesty, humility and a sense of humour.

Your own Parent Wish should be future focused and could include, for example, that your teenager:

- always seeks the truth
- always keeps their mind open to possibilities
- keeps good health and maintains the courage to face life's challenges
- is respectful of others' feelings and property
- is happy
- achieves their full potential in life
- is able to get along with others.

In developing your Parent Wish take time to ensure you have an accurate view of your teenager. While it is true that a parent knows their teenager better than anyone, it is also true that sometimes parents have an inaccurate or unrealistic understanding of the nature and ability of their teenager. It is important therefore to check the perception you have of your teenager with people in their life-world including, for example, other family members, friends or your teenager's teacher, school counsellor or sports coach. This will ensure the Parent Wish you have for your teenager is both realistic and achievable by your teenager.

"It's difficult to decide whether growing pains are something teenagers have, or are."
— A.S. Neil

I have the words 'self-knowledge', 'self-acceptance' and 'self-commitment' engraved on a crystal figurine that I keep on a bookshelf in my home. This is my 'Touchstone' to remind me and keep me grounded about what is important in my parenting role. I find that by regularly holding my touchstone and thinking about the words of my Parent Wish, especially at times when things aren't going so smoothly with my parenting, helps me to keep the inevitable day-to-day challenges of parenting a teenager in perspective. It helps to keep me focused on the big picture stuff — the lifelong wishes I have for my teenager, not the trials and tribulations of the day I am having with them. It is not of course necessary that you engrave your own touchstone. You might use some small item that reminds of your child or the bond between the two of you. Something perhaps from their earlier childhood when you had the natural closeness that comes with caring for a small child. Make your touchstone important to you. Keep it in a highly visible place to remind yourself of the purpose of your parenting. This will help to guide your thinking and action as you go about your day-to-day practice of parenting of your teenager.

"Children learn to smile from their parents."
— Shinichi Suzuki

Just as you need to gain knowledge, acceptance, and commitment on the journey with your teenager and have a Parent Wish to guide your parenting you also need to help your teenager on their journey. They will travel from childhood to adulthood as they get to know themselves ('the person they really are'), accept themselves, ('their strengths and limitations'), and commit themselves to be the best they can be in life.

My own research and experience in working with teenagers has shown that those who go on to become well-adjusted adults typically have a genuine understanding of themselves, are accepting of and comfortable with their strengths (gifts) as well as their limits, and are fully committed to developing those gifts and talents no matter what they are to be the very best they can be in life. These teenagers also usually display the personal qualities of responsibility, integrity, loyalty, dependability, commitment, humility, honesty, and have a sense of humour.

Taking care of yourself

To successfully parent your teenager on their journey from childhood to adulthood you will also need to take care of yourself. You need to work at maintaining your personal wellbeing — your feeling of inner contentment and being at peace with the world. Having a feeling of wellbeing will give you strength, hope and energy to keep parenting, especially through the difficult sometimes seemingly hopeless times.

"To understand your parents you must raise children yourself."
— Chinese Proverb

To achieve a sense of wellbeing you need to regularly find time just for you. This is your 'Parent Time'. It might be engaging in a favourite pastime such as reading or gardening, or a sporting or other physical activity, or just walking the dog. It could also be regularly going to your favourite place for time-out by yourself. What is important is that you make your Parent Time a sacred and high priority part of your weekly schedule. Maintaining your Parent Time will help keep you energised to parent your teenager with purpose, consistency and hope.

I strive to maintain my own personal wellbeing through a combination of daily physical exercise and spending my weekly Parent Time at my special place — a large rock ledge overlooking the ocean near where I live. The rock has special significance for me as it is where I often sat as a child. It is also the place from where my father's ashes were spread. Spending time once a week at my rock gives me time out from the inevitable day-to-day challenges of parenting my teenager. Sitting on the rock and thinking about the goals I have for my teenager in life helps me keep focused on my Parent Wish and not become weighed down and paralysed by a particular issue or current parenting challenge. I always come away from my rock focused on my Parent Wish and re-energised.

So make sure you find and maintain your weekly Parent Time at your special place or with your favourite activity and strive to make your life happy. Remember that being consistently confident, hopeful and enthusiastic about life is a key factor in effectively parenting your teenager. When you are at peace with yourself and the world it is more likely you will parent with

*CAUTION
THE WORLD HAS SHIFTED FOREVER —
STAY AHEAD*

purpose, confidence, hope and commitment. You then become a mirror for your teenager to see and model your positive life-enhancing behaviour and have confidence that they are being fully supported by a loving parent as they journey through the teenage years to adulthood.

Another very effective way of maintaining your commitment to parenting your teenager is to find a few minutes at the end of each day to identify, record and celebrate signs, no matter how seemingly small, that your teenager is growing in responsibility. This will give you encouragement and energy to start each day renewed and ready to continue to support your teenager on the rollercoaster ride through the teenage years.

Key things to remember

- Parenting a teenager requires purpose, creativity, determination, persistence, patience, hope and a sense of humour.
- You need a 'Parent Wish' to guide your parenting.
- Parenting is a journey of self-discovery for you and your teenager.
- You need to ensure your personal wellbeing and maintain confidence, hope and enthusiasm about life.
- You need to find and maintain your 'Parent Time' weekly.

Chapter

3

Being a teenager

"Some parents could do more for their children by not doing so much for them."
— anonymous

The teenage years from 13 to 19, also known as adolescence, is a time of extraordinary change both physically and emotionally. Physical changes occur more rapidly in adolescence than at any other time in life except the early growth spurt of infancy. Emotional changes are also unpredictable and complex at this time, leaving many teenagers (and their parents) confused and uncertain about themselves and life in general.

Adding to the confusion and uncertainty for both teenager and parent is the fact that research has now shown a teenager does not necessarily think like an adult on reaching puberty. A teenager's brain actually works differently to that of an adult. The part of the brain controlling planning, mood and impulse control does not, in many teenagers, mature until late adolescence or even into the early twenties. It would be incorrect then to think or to expect that a child can think like an adult simply because they have reached puberty.

Further adding to the complexity and challenges, research also shows that boys and girls are starting their adolescence earlier, finishing it much later and are more influenced by the media and technology than adolescents of a generation ago.

Little wonder then that a teenager growing up today is likely to be confused and uncertain, fluctuating between wanting freedom and at the same time still needing the security of their family. Little wonder also that a heavily media-influenced teenager is ever ready to challenge and reject the advice of a parent in favour of what they hear or see from someone else is the right way to live their life.

> "The young are always ready to give those who are older than themselves the full benefit of their inexperience."
>
> — anonymous

What is also known about adolescence is that your teenager will move through three distinct developmental stages or phases — early, middle and late adolescence — as they grow from childhood to adulthood. These stages will mean they have to confront and achieve a number of important developmental tasks before they become a well-adjusted adult. The tasks include forming and securing a positive identity, achieving independence from adults, establishing love objects outside the family, and finding a place in the world by establishing career direction and economic independence. There is no set beginning or length of time for each of these stages of development. Some adolescents experience difficulty with a particular stage, others experience difficulty with all stages, and some adolescents pass without difficulty through all stages of development.

Keep a cool head — it may be the only one for miles

While there is similarity in the developmental journey experienced by all teenagers it should be remembered that each teenager, as a consequence of their unique nature and life-world, experience a developmental journey different from anyone else. It is also important to remember that some teenagers will face additional challenges not common to most teenagers on the journey. Such challenges include those arising from a living in a dysfunctional family, having a learning disability or learning difficulty, having a psychological disorder, or having a particular cultural background. Many of these teenagers have difficulty coping and become troubled as they struggle to face particular life challenges in addition to those experienced by all teenagers.

"Be kind whenever possible. It is always possible."
— The 13th Dalai Lama

In early adolescence the onset of puberty signals a rapid change in the body of a teenager. During this developmental phase the main concern of a teenager is that they are like everyone else their age. They want to experience and believe that they are normal. While a teenager's physical appearance typically changes noticeably at this time they can also be emotionally unstable. One day they can be calm and act with maturity, the next they can be very moody, tearful, and generally behave immaturely with seemingly little or no change in their environment to indicate the cause.

It is during this time that patience and diplomacy is most required. Be extra patient with your teenager and let things that don't significantly endanger the realisation of your Parent Wish go. In other words 'only sweat the big stuff'. Stay involved and connected and always focus on their positives. Avoid comment about their physical appearance, don't over-control and give them space. Aim for your teenager to feel safe, valued and listened too.

During middle adolescence the main concern for your teenager is to form their own identity. At this time friendships become increasingly important. The authority of adults generally and in particular their parent, is questioned and in some instances rejected by the teenager. Keeping communication channels open and making sure your teenager feels connected is of paramount importance during middle adolescence. Listen and try to remain calm and positive regardless of the issue. When facing a challenging situation tell yourself to 'Take 60'. That is, not to react in any way either verbally or non verbally for 60 seconds. This will give you the time needed to decide how to react in a way that diffuses the situation and promotes a right constructive relationship with your teenager.

Try also to not use closed non-negotiable words such as 'forbid' and 'banned'. Instead, be prepared to discuss, listen, negotiate and/or compromise. Remember, however, that there also needs to be definite boundaries dividing the acceptable and unacceptable and that your role as parent is to be the leader of the family.

In late adolescence the major question for a teenager relates to discovering their identity and their place in the world. Typically, uncertainty and anxiety accompany your teenager's attempt to face questions about what the future holds for them — in particular, if they make poor choices and can't cope with new demands. They are also concerned about what significant people in their life, especially their parents, will think of them if they don't make a success of things.

Watch your "buttons" — your teenager will keep trying to push them

At this time your teenager needs to know that you will always be there for them and that you genuinely support their ambitions and plans. Typically at this time, teenagers begin to value their parents again and seek their support in making important decisions about their future direction.

"The face of a child can say it all, especially the mouth part of the face."
— Jack Hendy

It would not necessarily be right, however, to assume that at this transition time to adulthood your teenager automatically gains a clear direction for their life, especially their work life. Today's generation of teenagers have of necessity to deal with a world of unpredictable outcomes including changed economic, social and political conditions. Many things the previous generation took for granted are now not so certain and older traditions and patterns have become less useful as a template for life. Today's teenager will view their future work life quite differently to that of a teenager from the previous generation. A teenager today does not necessarily expect to commence full-time work or a career on completing school. Rather, they expect to work a number of part-time jobs. Current research predicts that today's teenagers can expect to work in at least six different careers during their life and that many teenagers will continue to live in their family home well into their twenties.

Without doubt a teenager today requires a new set of skills including knowing how to learn and having the capacity to make decisions and take choices about almost every aspect of their lives. To function effectively in today's world then, a teenager needs to *learn how to learn* and to be a versatile, quick and flexible thinker in today's ever-changing world.

As a part of the 'click and go' generation, today's teenagers are often impatient. Advances in technology have dramatically increased the speed of communication. Today's technologically smart teenager expects to be able to communicate instantly with anyone anywhere day or night. They no longer accept the advice of parents or other adults without question. They can access authoritative information about any topic they choose in an instant.

Keep parenting with patience

This expectation has led to the emergence of an impatient self-centred society increasingly demanding instant gratification.

Today's teenagers are also heavily influenced to grow up too quickly by the media. Magazines, films and television shape and influence a teenager, telling the teenager what they should think and when and how they should act. The potential significant influence of technology and the media on a teenager today is evident in the research showing that by the time a teenager has reached 15 years of age, they have spent 10,000 hours playing video games, 20,000 hours watching television and over 20,000 hours talking on the phone. This does not include hours listening to music, being on the internet, and using instant message systems, chat rooms and emails.

> "Some parents really bring their children up; others let them down."
> — anonymous

Yet in all this world of rapid change it is important to remember again that some things don't change. No matter what generation they are from teenagers must still pass through the developmental phases of every human's journey to adulthood. What does change is the significant influence of technology and the media on a teenager. Given this influence it is vital that you encourage your teenager to discuss what they are seeing and hearing via the various media and outlets they use so as to gain an informed view on issues of importance in their life. This may mean a rapid update in world and local affairs and use of technology for some parents! *(Smile. It'll do you good!)*

Key things to remember

- A teenager faces both predictability and unpredictability during the teenage years.
- A teenager moves through developmental phases and needs to master developmental tasks on their journey to adulthood.
- A teenager's unique nature and life-world makes them like no other teenager.

- A teenager's behaviour is significantly influenced by technology and the visual and print media.

- As parent you need to be purposeful, supportive, diplomatic and patient with your teenager on their journey to adulthood.

Chapter

4

Parenting with purpose and patience

> "Where parents do too much for their children the children will not do much for themselves."
> — anonymous

As I emphasised earlier, to effectively parent your teenager you need to be a full-time parent with a purpose — a purpose to work consistently and patiently at achieving your Parent Wish. Your approach should always aim at helping your teenager come to understand themselves, accept themselves and to commit themselves to be the very best they can be in their life.

Yet even with this approach, the only certainty you can look forward to as you go about parenting your teenager is uncertainty. Your teenager is a multi-faceted marvel likely at one time to be selfish, narrow minded, difficult and challenging, and at other perhaps unexpected times to be spontaneous, affectionate and a pleasure to have around.

It can be helpful to remember the saying: 'It takes a village to raise a child'. Your parenting effectiveness will be maximised by regularly seeking feedback from those who know you in your life-world on their perception of your parenting style, and checking from time to time on how your teenager is reacting and dealing with that parenting style. Be willing to modify your parenting approach and expectations if there are any unexpected changes or as your teenager demonstrates increased responsibility. Always be alert to seize any opportunity that will lead them to a deeper self-knowledge.

STAY AHEAD — THE WORLD HAS SHIFTED FOREVER (AND WILL KEEP SHIFTING!)

In essence, you are aiming to maintain a 'right relationship' with your teenager. A right relationship exists when you and your teenager understand and agree on the different roles and responsibilities you both have in the family. As a parent, you are the leader of the family and your teenager is a member of the family. Your role and responsibility is to ensure their wellbeing and safety and to lead and support them on their journey through the teenage years to adulthood. Your teenager's role is to be a much-loved, valued, respected and responsible individual within the family.

It is important that you both understand and accept these roles. And you as a parent must lead. Your effectiveness in parenting your teenager depends on your leadership.

It is likely that the structure of the family you lead today is quite different from the typical two-parent family structure supported by a network of nearby living relations of a generation ago. It doesn't matter however whether your family is two-parent, single-parent, or blended. It is a family, and what happens in a family is important.

> Parents must get across the idea that "I love you always, but sometimes I do not love your behaviour."
> — Amy Vinderbelt

Your family will function best if you all follow the 'Family View'. This is the set of rules by which your family operates. You should not be afraid to set rules. Living without rules provokes uncertainty and anxiety in a teenager and it makes it harder for them to learn how to achieve the balance between getting what they want and respecting the needs of others. Try to involve every member of the family in developing the Family View as this will help them to understand and maintain the principles behind the rules.

While the rules you decide on will be influenced by your beliefs and values and particular situation, they should be as few in number as possible and 'bottom line' to ensure the functioning of the family. Bottom line rules could be thought of as 'old fashioned family values' — the fundamental, unchanging core values your family will always stand for. Rules should, for example, address personal physical safety, personal respect, respect for the property of an individual, daily routines and communication when away from home.

Rules should be consistently applied and not seem to change arbitrarily. Consistency allows your teenager to make predictions about their world. Yet there should also be enough flexibility so rules can be tested, challenged and changed as your teenager grows and demonstrates the ability to be responsible and self-governing. Rules should not be vague and open to interpretation. You need to be clear and precise in describing what to do or not to do. Don't assume, however, that your teenager will easily know the rules and how to behave in a responsible self-governing way. You need to teach your teenager how to behave responsibly in relation to the rules and check that they accurately understand the rules and the consequences for failing to abide by them. Be firm and consistent with rule enforcement.

"Parents who are afraid to put their foot down usually have children who step on their toes."
— Chinese Proverb

Parenting style is key to effective parenting. Common parenting styles can be broadly categorised into three types:

- the Boot Camp Commander
- the Rescue Helicopter Pilot
- the Personal Life Coach.

A parent using the *Boot Camp Commander* style of parenting commands and directs the life of their teenager. They typically issue orders and threats and take ownership of an issue or problem. This sends a hidden message to their teenager that 'You cannot think, and have to be bossed around and told what to do'. This control approach is not preferred as it is manipulative and does not promote individuality with personal responsibility.

A parent using the *Rescue Helicopter Pilot* style of parenting typically hovers over their teenager, taking on the responsibility of the teenager to protect them from any negative feelings. The hidden message sent to their teenager is 'You're fragile and can't make it without me'. This rescuer approach is also not preferred as it does not let a teenager experience real life or promote personal responsibility.

A parent using the *Personal Life Coach* style of parenting provides their teenager with messages of personal worth and strength by helping them explore alternatives and allowing them to make their own decisions. Whenever possible they let life's natural consequences be the teacher for their teenager. This is clearly the style of parenting a teenager most preferred as it promotes responsibility and ownership of a problem or issue by the teenager. While there will be times when of necessity your parenting style will need to be more directive, at life-threatening times for example, always try to return to and use the Personal Life Coach approach to parenting your teenager.

Coaching your teenager includes telling them often of your love for them and your confidence in their ability to make good choices and to be responsible. Tell them also that while you will always love them you do not necessarily like or accept inappropriate or irresponsible behaviour by them.

MAINTAIN CONSISTENCY

Of course, while having a warm positive relationship with your teenager is ideal there will be times when you will have to make unpopular decisions. Although your teenager may dislike you for the decision, be confident that they will not stop loving you. Remember, you are *their parent not their pal*. In that role, you also need to keep in mind that you are only in control of yourself. It is impossible to control the thoughts, words, decisions, behaviours and actions of your teenager. The best you can do is set up situations in which your teenager either decides it is best to do as asked, or experiences the logical consequences of their actions, just as they will in their adult life. It is likely, however, that your teenager will be more cooperative when they feel they have some control over their own situation.

It is important also to remember that thoughts add shape to our reality and our action. So if you parent your teenager with a *closed*, limiting mindset that regards them as being lazy, ungrateful, self-centred and needing close control and direction you will not have a 'right relationship' and it is unlikely your teenager will behave responsibly. If, on the other hand, you parent your teenager with an *open*, enabling mindset that sees your teenager as being worthy and capable of demonstrating responsibility, it is likely they will behave responsibly and you will enjoy a mutually beneficial relationship with them.

"Where parents do too much for their children the children will not do much for themselves."
— anonymous

A healthy self-concept, or self-esteem, is the key to being able to learn and be effective in home, school and eventually out in the real world. A teenager who shows responsibility typically has a healthy self-concept. Self-esteem is developed in a teenager when they live in a supportive, predictable and reliable environment that communicates belief in and respect for them, celebrates their successes and achievements, and is excited for them and with them about their hopes and dreams in life.

Self-esteem involves knowing how you feel about yourself and plays a significant role in almost everything you do. It is the building block to becoming a well-adjusted happy adult. People with high self-esteem, those who feel they are likeable and lovable, have better relationships. They have positive beliefs about themselves, feel confident and optimistic about the future and are more likely to ask for help and support from friends and family when they need it. They are also people who feel energetic about things, believe they can accomplish goals and solve problems and feel proud, satisfied and happy with their achievements.

Teenagers with high self-esteem do better in school and tend to have better relationships with peers and adults. They find it easier to deal with mistakes and disappointments, feel happier, and are more likely to stick with something until they succeed. Typically a teenager with high self-esteem uses positive self-confident signalling words such as:

- 'I am capable.'
- 'I can do it.'
- 'I will succeed.'

Teenagers with low self-esteem feel they are not a worthwhile person. They typically have negative thoughts about themselves and what they can do, have little confidence or hope in the future and stop trying to achieve things. A teenager with low self-esteem typically uses negative self-effacing words such as:

- 'I am useless.'
- 'I am stupid.'
- 'I always fail.'

If your teenager has low self-esteem encourage them to listen to their self-talk and replace negative critical thoughts with positive ones. Self-talk is the conversation we have with ourselves in our head and something we all do no matter how old or young we are. Encourage your teenager to focus on their strengths rather than their shortcomings by striving:

- to aim for accomplishments rather than perfection
- to accept that everyone makes mistakes

- to view mistakes as learning opportunities
- to recognise what can and can't change
- to set realistic achievable goals about what they would like to accomplish, make a plan, stick with it and celebrate their achievements along the journey.

Every time you show your teenager through your actions that you know they can be responsible and that you expect them to be responsible you are building their self-esteem. You can further help build your teenager's self-esteem by using a love and logic approach to parenting. First, you need to create and use enforceable statements. These are statements you make to your teenager which you can and will follow through. Such statements become enforceable limits, which allow you to fulfil your role as parent without the use of anger, lectures, threats or repeated warnings. Setting firm limits increases the likelihood your teenager will be more confident and responsible. Describing what you will do or allow sets a limit. Telling your teenager what they should or shouldn't do, is likely to be challenged and resisted. The second step in building your teenager's self-esteem is to give them as many choices as seems reasonable within the set limit. This approach will encourage them to deal with their particular issue or problem without immediately referring to you to fix it. The third step in building your teenager's self-esteem is to allow, except in cases of life threatening danger, natural and logical consequences, to do the teaching.

Examples of love and logic enforceable statements include:

- 'I'll be happy to drive you to your friends home as soon as your room is in order.'
- 'I'll allow use of the phone when I feel the privilege is not being abused.'
- 'I'll listen to you as soon as your voice is as calm and respectful as mine.'

You can also help build your teenager's self-esteem by giving them a method to solve problems. Just as a touchstone will help you keep on track to achieve your Parent Wish, so too will a touchstone inscribed with the words *Knowledge, Acceptance, Commitment* help your teenager solve most problems they will encounter on the journey. Any symbol of importance to your teenager can become their touchstone to use to help solve a problem in their life. When your teenager is facing a problem support them by first showing them you understand and are empathetic about their problem saying, for example, 'That sounds difficult' or 'I bet that feels terrible'. Immediately ask the question, 'Have you been to your touchstone and thought about what you need to know about the problem, what you have to accept about

the problem and what commitment you will have to make to solve the problem?' This lets them know you have confidence in their ability to think and it also lets them know who owns the problem.

After listening to any suggestions your teenager might have to solve their problem ask if they would like to know what others have done. Follow up any option your teenager might offer with statements such as, 'How do you think that would work?' Show them support for their thinking by saying, for example, 'Sounds like you have some good ideas going' or 'I'd like to know how that turns out for you, good luck'. This approach gives your teenager the message that while you are very pleased to help them, the problem is in the end theirs to solve.

"The art of dealing with children might be defined as knowing what not to say."
— A.S. Neil

But of course, your parenting journey being akin to that roller-coaster ride we have already talked about, it is to be expected then that from time to time the behaviour of your teenager will frustrate and anger you no matter how hard you have tried to parent well. After all, anger is a normal human emotion. How you manage your frustration and anger will very much influence your relationship and your ongoing effectiveness in parenting your teenager.

Anger comes in different degrees, dependent on whether the action of someone is perceived to be accidental or deliberate. The key to managing your teenager's anger is to effectively manage your own anger. Teenagers copy behaviour, so to be the best teacher of anger management techniques, you need to model your own anger management effectively. The extra benefit of being a good role model is that you will practise for yourself effective anger management and end up a better person as the journey continues.

You manage your anger by first being aware of the event or situation that provokes anger. This will help you to prepare for, diffuse or avoid angry settings. Recognising the degree of your anger will also help you manage the powerful emotional responses you will have to it that can interfere with clear thinking. Try to track your level of consciousness such as increased muscle tension, holding your breath, breathing, quickly raising your voice or talking over people.

One of the best ways to manage your anger is to be an effective communicator and listener. It is especially important to keep communication channels open with your teenager. Studies have shown that teenagers who can communicate with their parents are much happier, feel more connected with their family, and are more self-confident and resilient in facing the changes and challenges of life in general than those who have limited or no communication with their parent.

"Encourage your teenager to express disagreement with you so long as they can explain why without resorting to 'whatever'!"

— Jeff Kemp

Choose the right moment to communicate with your teenager remembering that it is best to resolve problems cooperatively with cool heads. Be conscious of your tone of voice, facial expressions, demeanour and body language. Don't accuse, insult or talk down to your teenager by using comments beginning with, for example:

- 'You must ...'
- 'You won't ...'
- 'That's stupid ...'

Instead, show your teenager you are listening to them by being attentive — listen with affection. Try to put yourself in their shoes. Don't argue or change the subject. Have an attitude that invites them to tell you more. Give a nod of the head and make eye contact without challenging. Allow your teenager to express themselves without reacting judgmentally to what they say. Try not to over-react or under-react, and focus on the present not the past. Resist being drawn into an argument or power struggle with them. Explaining or reasoning does not work in this situation. Your teenager is not interested in facts and logic. They are more interested in seeing you give up. The best approach is to neutralise the argument by using one-liners such as:

- 'I respect you too much to argue.'
- 'I know.'
- 'I bet it feels bad.'
- 'What a bummer.'
- 'Could be.'
- 'How sad.'

There will always be times when you make mistakes and don't get it right in spite of all your efforts to have a right relationship with your teenager. Never give up on parenting them. Everyone makes mistakes and has good and not-so-good days. At difficult, seemingly hopeless times, go to your touchstone, hold it and reflect on the words that make up your Parent Wish. This will help you put the unpredictable daily teenager-challenging episodes in perspective, enable you to keep the end in mind and focused. Remember also to maintain a sense of humour. Laugh often at yourself and with your teenager over the ridiculous situations you sometimes get into, always keep humour upbeat, never sarcastic, and remember — *'the parent who laughs, lasts'!*

Finally, don't try to be perfect. Do try to be better. If you are unsure about something talk to other parents, your partner, friends and family or seek professional advice.

Key things to remember

- As a parent you need to lead and parent mindfully and with purpose.
- As a parent you need to establish and maintain the 'Family View'.
- Behaviour that needs to be learned needs to be taught.
- Rules worth having are worth enforcing.
- It's how rules are enforced that makes the difference.

- You need to adopt a personal life coach approach to parenting your teenager.

- Using a love and logic approach to parenting builds self-esteem in your teenager.

- Listening and communicating with your teenager builds a healthy right relationship.

- Maintaining a sense of humour strengthens the relationship with your teenager.

Chapter

5

Teen topics

The wide variety of issues you can possibly face as a parent of a teenager is endless, and dictated by the circumstances of your life, the personalities of yourself, and your teenager. Most will be positive experiences that become a part of your shared history of the teenage years — the things that both your teenager and yourself will look back on in future years with a wry smile and a healthy laugh. Some, however, such as depression, self-harm, and suicide can have obvious serious consequences if not handled with purpose and patience. In this chapter, I have selected a few important teen topics that may need special parenting attention, and provided some thoughts on each as to what they mean and how you might cope with them.

Friends

An important developmental task faced by a teenager as they grow from childhood to adulthood is to form attachments with people outside of the family. It is to be expected then that your teenager will become more independent and that people their own age — their peers — will play a greater role in their life. Most people are influenced by their peers because they want to be included, to do what others they admire do and be like them. Peer pressure then is a normal aspect of a teenager's life and is most important during middle adolescence.

What to do

While many parents are understandably fearful of the potential negative influence of peer pressure on their teenager, peers can also have a profoundly positive influence. Through your teenager's peer group they can learn to socialise, find acceptance and friendship, practise getting along with the opposite sex, learn to give and take, and gain good advice and new life experiences. Peers can also set good examples for each other, such as being committed to do their best at school or sport.

You can help develop your teenager's self-confidence and coping skills with friends by first allowing them to see how you successfully cope in different social situations. You can also involve them in variety of social situations such as sports or interest groups outside school, or you might rehearse and role play with them specific situations they might find difficult, and by building their self-confidence through praising them when they do things well.

Encouraging your teenager to accept an invitation to a party can also build their social competence. To ensure they enjoy a party in safety speak with a parent of the teenager hosting the party to find out how many will be attending the party, how the party will be supervised, if alcohol will be available, a phone or mobile contact number of an adult supervising the party and the expected finish time of the party so you can arrange to collect your teenager.

If you are hosting a party for your teenager make entrance to the party by invitation only. Ensure the invitation clearly states a start and finish time and whether or not alcohol is provided, permitted, or be brought by attendees. Advise your neighbours and the police about the party, arrange adult supervision, have emergency numbers including a taxi service, ambulance and police with you, and encourage parents to collect their teenager at the end of the party.

While involvement with peers can be a very healthy part of a teenager's development, teenagers who lack confidence or have low self-esteem can be pressured into doing something they are not comfortable with, such as binge drinking. Your teenager can resist peer pressure by strengthening their self-esteem, to see themselves as a person of worth, and by encouraging them to choose their friends wisely. If they choose friends with similar interests it will be less likely they will be pressured into doing things they know are wrong. Encourage them also to pay attention to their own feelings of what is the right or the wrong thing to do, to stay away from peers who put pressure on them and to speak to a trusted adult, such as a school counsellor, if they are finding it difficult to resist peer pressure.

In sum, your goal should be to help your teenager discover and develop their unique gifts to ensure high self-esteem and confidence to develop friendships with like-minded peers.

Body image

Body image is what your teenager sees in their mind's eye when they think about their appearance. It is their perception of their physical body and how they feel others perceive it. It may be an image that does not relate strongly to how you see their body.

As teenagers today are constantly bombarded by media images of flawless people that seem real, normal and attainable, it is understandable that many teenagers chase the attainment of a non-existent perfect body. They think that to feel good about themselves they need to change the way they look. Such a belief can lead a teenager to engage in unhealthy choices resulting in eating disorders and low self-esteem.

What to do

Rather than have your teenager think they need to change how they look or act to feel good about themselves you should aim to help them change the way they see their body and what they think about themselves. The more comfortable they feel about themselves the more confident and attractive they will appear to themselves.

Encourage them to realise that their body is unique to them, no matter what shape, size or colour, and that there are some things about themselves such as their height or shoe size that they can't change and need to accept. Tell them that different people are different shapes and sizes, that some people are naturally thin and others aren't, that thin isn't necessarily healthy, and that they need to find and maintain a weight that's within the normal range for them.

Don't be obsessive about food or dieting yourself. Provide healthy nutritious food and allow food to be a source of pleasure. You could aim to make eating together once a week a family ritual. If your teenager continues to have a major concern with their body image seek professional advice and support. If they wish to change and can, encourage them to set goals for themselves and keep track of their progress until they reach their goal. For example, the goal of keeping fit can be achieved if they follow a regular exercise plan and eat nutritious foods. You can help them achieve their goal by having only nutritious food in the home, by not talking negatively about their weight or promoting the good looks of thin people, by encouraging them to exercise regularly, and by complimenting them on their effort and determination to stick with their plan to achieve their goal.

In sum, your teenager will have and maintain a good body image if they have high self-esteem, understand and accept their body type, and commit themselves to living a healthy lifestyle.

Depression

We all have our good and not-so-good days. Everyone feels angry or sad at times. It is part of being human. Depression, however, is not just going through a tough time. A teenager is showing the symptoms of depression when they feel sad, down and miserable most of the time and find it hard to cope from day to day. They typically lose interest in things they used to enjoy, seem to have less energy, find it difficult to concentrate, have trouble eating and sleeping, have low self-esteem, and seem to have little enjoyment in their lives.

What to do

Depression usually results from problems of loss. It is important not to ignore your teenager's feelings or dismiss their feelings with comments such as 'Wake up to yourself, you are worrying about nothing'. This is likely to make them feel that no-one understands them and that they are alone in the world. Be available for them and take time to listen when they want to talk about their feelings, and strengthen their self-esteem by encouraging them to do things you know they are good at or enjoy and to talk to someone they trust such as a friend, family member, teacher or school counsellor. If you are concerned your teenager is not responding to attempts to help them fight the depression then seek professional help from a registered psychologist. If your teenager feels they don't need help, tell them that you are concerned and need help to cope and you want them to come with you to see someone.

Self-harm

Self-harm means to deliberately harm or injure oneself without wanting to commit suicide. Some teenagers start self-harming when they are frustrated or depressed, extremely anxious or feeling trapped because of a certain situation in their lives. It is seen as a way of coping with inner pain and is often linked to low self-esteem and a feeling of being overwhelmed by intense emotions. These emotions typically include a feeling of being dissociated from everything around them.

What to do

Often a teenager who self-harms has difficulty coping with and talking about their emotions and believes that they are not coping. The self-harming can make them feel better so may not see that there any negative effects. Tell them that cuts sometimes become infected and turn to scars and that they may go too far and cause a severe injury leading to death. Give your teenager different strategies to use when they feel like self-harming, including finding a distraction that works, developing better coping skills, talking to someone they trust, and making a personal decision to stop the behaviour and remain focused and positive about life to avoid relapsing. Keep self-harming instruments such as razors and knives in a secure place at home and ensure that any wound doesn't become infected. Try to focus their mind on something other than the inner pain by occupying their time with creative activities such as painting or writing and encouraging them to have a healthy lifestyle, including healthy eating, physical fitness and overall personal wellbeing. If you or your teenager feels their self-harming is getting dangerous seek the advice of a registered psychologist, your family doctor, school counsellor or government health agency.

Suicide

Whereas teenagers usually have the resilience to bounce back from depression some teenagers, especially those without a support network of family and friends, feel isolated, worthless and disconnected from their life-world. These teenagers are at increased risk of suicide.

Suicide among teenagers is most often triggered by a major stressful event, such as perceived failure at school or in life generally, a broken relationship, the death of a loved one, or a major family conflict. Signs that a teenager is thinking about suicide include talking about suicide or death in general, withdrawing from family and friends, losing desire for favourite things, giving away belongings and self-destructive behaviours.

What to do

The best way to help your teenager if they are at risk of suicide is to look for warning signs that they are having suicidal thoughts. Keep the communication channels open and if you are concerned ask your teenager. Say, for example, 'Lately, I've heard you saying that life had no purpose and that you might as well be dead. Can you tell me why you are feeling this way?' If your teenager doesn't feel comfortable talking with you, suggest a person they respect such as the family doctor or school counsellor. If your teenager will not speak to someone get help from a registered psychologist, your local government mental health department, or seek professional advice yourself on how best to handle the situation.

Sexuality

Sexuality is a complex aspect of our personality and self. It refers to sexual feelings as well as behaviour. It is important to remember that sexuality is a vital aspect of a teenager's life and that a teenager who goes through puberty has the same hormones and the same hormonal drive as adults.

It often takes years for a teenager to grow into their sexuality. During this time many teenagers feel confused over their feelings and attractions. While most teenagers come to identify themselves as heterosexual, some identify with homosexuality, and still others identify themselves as being bisexual. It is important to remember that the human race is full of subtle and profound differences and that sexuality is just one part of the person.

What to do

Many parents worry about teenager sexuality. Unsure of what to do or say they hope their teenager is educated appropriately in health education programs at school. However, studies have shown when parents are open about discussing sexuality their teenager is less likely to engage in risky sexual behaviour. It is therefore important for you to talk openly and honestly with your teenager about the whole area of relationships, knowing that the more knowledge your teenager has the more they are effectively equipped to make good healthy choices.

One possible way to initiate such discussion is to ask about what is being said at school about relationships and sex, saying that you need to know that they are safe. Ensure your teenager knows that relationships should not be forced or unpleasant experiences, that good relationships involve mutual respect, honesty and trust and that they need to know how to avoid unsafe situations. If you discover your teenager has been engaging in risky behaviour do not over-react, threaten or blame your teenager. Try to remain calm and assure your teenager you will never abandon them and that you will support them in assessing all options available to them.

If you experience difficulty in communicating freely with your teenager in regard to sexuality give them specific reading material and/or appropriate website addresses or encourage them to confide in a trusted adult. It is vital at this time of development for a teenager to have the support and understanding as well as guidance from their parent. Remember your teenager is the same person regardless of sexuality.

Drugs and alcohol

A drug is any chemical compound or substance that when taken into the body changes the way we feel, the way we perceive things and the way the body works. Drugs come from a range of sources both naturally occurring and man made. There are three main types of drugs, classified according to the effect the drug has on the central nervous system. These are depressants, stimulants and hallucinogens.

Common depressants include alcohol, barbiturates, cannabis and heroin. These drugs slow down the functions of the central nervous system. Stimulants include caffeine in coffee, tea and cola drinks, nicotine in tobacco and amphetamines. Stimulants act on the central nervous system to speed up the messages going to and from the brain. Hallucinogens affect a person's perception of things.

What to do

Your teenager is growing up in a drug-taking society. And since the teenage years is a time of experimentation and testing limits it is likely your teenager will experiment with drugs. It is important to remember that while there is no approach to parenting that will guarantee a teenager will never touch either legal or illegal drugs the strongest antidote known for alcohol and substance misuse is for a teenager to feel connected to others who genuinely care for them and to have the possibility of a fulfilling life.

A teenager may experiment with drugs and drinking for a number of reasons, including curiosity, boredom, peer pressure or the need to feel part of the group, to cope with feelings of depression or stress or for excitement. Parents typically worry about their teenager becoming hooked on drugs. There is, however, no support for the theory that if a teenager tries a so-called soft drug — for example, marijuana — that it will only be a matter of time before they progress to hard drugs such heroin. The real threat to a teenager's health is the use of social drugs such as tobacco and alcohol.

While there is no easy way to tell if your teenager is taking drugs or abusing alcohol, signs include uncharacteristic behaviour such as outbursts of anger toward others, mood swings, significant changes in physical appearance, the disappearance of money or household items, and a sudden change to a new group of friends.

If you think your teenager is taking drugs do not react immediately and jump to conclusions. Give yourself time to think through what is happening and to inform yourself about drugs. Do not exaggerate or make things up. Foster a close open and trusting relationship with your teenager and discuss your concern at a time when you are both in a reasonable mood. Tell them of your concern for their wellbeing and try to separate their behaviour from them as an individual.

Ensure the communication channels remain open and keep them connected and involved with the family. At the right time say something that opens up the subject in an easy non-threatening way such as 'Is everything OK? Lately, you don't seem to be yourself'. Reassure them by telling them that while you might not like nor accept their behaviour you will always love them an be there to support them. Encourage positive self-talk to build their self-esteem and model a healthy living lifestyle based on nutritious eating, regular exercise and caring respectful relationships within the family.

Don't try and scare your teenager off drugs. Have open and honest discussions and educate your teenage on what is likely to happen if they use drugs or abuse alcohol. Ensure they are aware of the effect on family relationships, their education and their future career prospects. Have a Family View rule about what is acceptable behaviour in regard to drugs and in particular to alcohol. If you remain concerned that your teenager is heavily involved in drugs, seek immediate professional advice and support from the relevant government department or specialist agency within your local community.

Technology

For many parents, technology is like magic. To your teenager technology is an integral part of their life. Teenagers are very comfortable living in a world dominated by sophisticated integrated technologies, including for example, computers, the internet, smart phones, multiple television channels, portable music players, and game consoles.

What to do

While the use of technology offers great potential to enrich lives through access to information and communication it also puts your teenager at risk of exposure to age-inappropriate content and risky social contacts. The fact is that when your teenager uses text messaging, chat rooms or interactive websites they can't be sure who they are communicating with. Regrettably, advances in technology are being used by sex offenders to prey on and exploit teenagers. As parent you must manage your teenager's use of technology, particularly in communicating with others and when engaging in social networking via the internet.

Management of your teenager's use of the internet should include keeping the computer in a room the whole family has access to, installing filtering and/or computer blocking software, and setting clear family rules for internet use. Ensure you are able to randomly check your teenager's email and that your teenager knows the importance of not sharing passwords, giving their personal details including photos to someone they meet in a chat room, and that they know the legal ramifications of what they say and do online.

Most parents these days provide their teenager with a mobile phone as a way of maintaining contact at particular times in the day and in emergency situations. You can manage your teenager's use of a mobile phone by arranging with the telephone provider to block all services not required, by stressing the importance of not giving out personal details and by not responding to any message from someone unknown to them. Talk to your teenager about the appropriate use of a camera phone and of the need to record and report the number of persistent calls from unknown people to you for reporting to the police. Ensure your teenager also knows that all they say in text messages and emails can be kept and that they know the possible legal ramifications of what they say and do via their phone.

Chapter

6

Teen scenarios

This section is designed to allow the reader to connect with the values and thoughts developed from the opening chapters of this book and to provide practice in effective parenting — being your teenager's parent, not their pal. It is presented as a series of 25 teen scenarios in which you are asked to imagine you are the parent dealing with that teenager. Some scenarios may be similar to something you or a another parent you know have experienced, they may be things you are yet to face, or they may be episodes you might never have to come across. These scenarios are, however, very real and while you may not wish to come across some of them, they are all drawn from real life and illustrate the trials of many ordinary parents coping with the many twists and turns a life can throw at you. Whatever the case, as you read each scenario think about the possible emotions being experienced by both the parent and the child, the purpose of the behaviour shown by the teenager, and the possible consequences and ways of encouraging responsible behaviour. A recommended action plan follows each scenario as a guide to how it might be handled in line with the philosophy of this book.

Broken-hearted

You are a single mother with one son aged 15 years. Your ex-husband has rejected your son and has made no contact with you or your son for almost two years. Your son has always been strong-willed, impulsive, and at times difficult to manage. He is an insulin-dependent diabetic. The efforts of you and his doctor to ensure he remains attentive to the management of his own health makes little impression with him. He has had to be hospitalised a number of times to stabilise his physical functioning. The lack of concern he shows for his own health is of ongoing concern to you.

As your work is stressful and involves varying times away from home you enrolled him in a boarding college. He fails to adjust to boarding school and on the recommendation of the boarding school principal is enrolled in a medium-sized coeducational college close to your home. With the support of the college counsellor your son makes a smooth transition to his new college. Initial school reports note a quiet, somewhat aloof, reflective student who does not consistently apply himself to his schoolwork.

Over time you have experienced great difficulty managing his challenging behaviour. Six months ago he met his first girlfriend. In recent days the close relationship was ended abruptly by the girl when she told your son she did not want a close relationship and that she wanted to just be friends. This news deeply upset your son.

Yesterday you received a telephone call from the police reporting that your son had been captured on closed circuit television standing on the rail tracks near the local railway station.

Action plan

Given your son's demonstrated lack of care for his personal wellbeing, his history of difficult impulsive behaviour, and his recent depression and reaction over the break-up with his girlfriend, you need to quickly enact a comprehensive action to support your son at this time.

Seek immediate psychiatric support, which could include a period of hospitalisation to monitor and stabilise his mental and physical health. At the same time work in partnership with his school counsellor to discreetly monitor his demeanour regularly through the day and to rebuild his self-esteem.

Bush lawyer

Your youngest son commenced secondary school this year, enrolled at the same school attended several years ago by his brother. You have been divorced for five years and have a less than favourable relationship with your son's father; disagreeing on most things, especially about the parenting of your children.

For some time now your son has been complaining about the teachers at his school, saying that they have been unjustly picking on him, wrongly accusing him of things he didn't do, and excluding him from class for what he regards as minor behaviour issues. He tells you he wants to change school as he believes all the teachers at his present school are against him and that he could have a fresh start at a nearby school attended by his friends from primary school. The school has contacted you to express concern about the lack of respect your son is showing teachers and other adults in the school community.

While you are open to your son changing school, his father is opposed, saying he needs to behave himself and stay at his current school. You attend a meeting with his teachers arranged by the school guidance counsellor and learn that while your son is a capable, articulate student, his behaviour is unacceptable as he challenges decisions of teachers and refuses to accept responsibility for his behaviour. Moreover, he constantly criticises the teaching ability of the majority of his teachers and rules made by the school administrators. You are also told that he seemingly likes having other students as an audience for his complaints and that according to his primary school reports he displayed similar behaviour in his final year of school.

Action plan

Your son's behaviour since commencing secondary school is a continuation of the way he behaved in primary school. Allowing him to change school will only transfer the problem to another site. The negative abrasive attitude he is presently displaying is no different to the way he related to his teacher and school administrators in his final year of primary school. Your son could also be using the discord between you and his father to more easily achieve his goal.

At this time you need to put aside the personal differences you have with his father and agree that your son will be staying at his present school and that you will work in partnership with his teachers and school administrators to ensure he maintains right relations with them. Your agreement with his school should include regular communication with them as to your son's attitude and demeanour and his overall progress.

Tell your son of the decision you and his father have made about which secondary school he will attend and your determination to work in partnership with his teachers to monitor his behaviour. Remind him of the consistent comments made by teachers about his academic potential, his keen sense of justice and his ability to communicate as a speaker. Be alert and praise him for maintaining correct respectful relationships with everyone he meets and by being less judgemental of people. Encourage him to further develop his skills as an orator by joining the school debating team or similar group within the community.

'Big T'

You are a single father with a 13-year-old son. You were a professional football player and up until this year coached the team in which your son played. Your son is physically well developed for his age and people often mistakenly think him to be much older than his actual age. To your great delight your son was selected in successive regional representative football teams, with coaches reporting that he had great potential as a player.

You are struggling financially, however, and finding it difficult to secure permanent work. You become extremely frustrated and angry with your son when you receive reports from school that he has been bullying other students and not applying himself to his schoolwork. While your son has always struggled with traditional schoolwork your frustration boils over when you learn he has missed a number of representative football team training sessions and is close to being cut from the team. You react by telling him he is lazy and useless and will never amount to anything in life. You feel particularly upset as you believe you are trying your best under difficult circumstances to give your son the opportunity to realise his sporting potential and become a professional football player.

You reluctantly accept a school recommendation for your son to complete a wilderness adventure-based personal development program, thinking that it would be a waste of time. Yet you discover that your son enjoyed the program immensely and you are pleasantly surprised with the program report that your son was voted unanimously by other program participants and program personnel as the most able and popular participant in the program. The report also regarded your son to be a sincere reflective boy, 'a gentle giant', who responded well to praise and confided that he didn't really want to be thought of by others as a bully.

Action plan

Your son's performance on the wilderness adventure program has revealed that he is not a careless bully but rather a teenager with great outdoor skills and leadership ability. His size and difficulty with the traditional school curriculum has led to him adopting the unwanted role of disengaged student and bully. While his diminishing interest in football causes you great distress your son is not you and may not have the same ambition to become a professional player even if he has the ability. Care should be taken to select school subjects with significant practical hands-on components, and initial discussions held in regard to a future career in an outdoor trade, horticulture or with the parks and wildlife service. Above all, your son needs to experience your unconditional love for him and your support for him to develop his unique gifts in life.

Coming out

You and your husband have a 16-year-old son. Yours is a caring family that places emphasis on maintaining strong ties with the extended family. Your son is also family oriented and regularly communicates with his grandparents, uncles and aunties and cousins. He is a gentle sensitive boy and is well liked and accepted by all members of the family.

Recently your son disclosed to you and your husband that he was homosexual. You reassure him of your love for him and his worth as a person and respected member of the family.

While school reports have consistently reported him to be a student of above average ability with a particular gift in written expression your son has become very unhappy at school.

You learn that he has been the brunt of taunts and bullying and you decide to change his school as the school had seemingly ignored your call to stop the bullying and ensure your son's wellbeing. Sadly, soon after commencing at his new school the name calling and bullying recommences. Your son reacts by progressively disengaging with school providing a variety of reasons for not going to school. The school eventually contacts you regarding his absenteeism.

His school offers support by giving an assurance that they would adopt and follow through with a zero tolerance of bullying and by giving your son an extension of time to complete work assignments now long overdue in all subjects. At the time your son develops irregular sleep patterns staying up into the early morning hours and sleeping though the day.

Action plan

Maintaining your son's connectedness within the family and with school and building his self-esteem, interpersonal skills and resilience should be the key goals of the support plan.

Seek the support of your close knit immediate and extended family to reassure him of his worth and importance both as an individual and a member of the family. You can also work in partnership with his school to build self-esteem and social skills so as to minimise the potential for him to be bullied at school. Finally, seek the support of a respected teacher or adult outside of school to encourage and to mentor him with the development of his writing skills. Your son could also be encouraged to join a writing club outside of school with the aim of developing his writing skills and building his social skills.

Cyber bully

Your daughter is in her second year of secondary school. While her grades in the first year were quite promising they have since dropped across the board. Your daughter regards being thought of as a leader as very important and appears to be popular with her peers.

One weekend you receive an irate phone call from a parent of a girl in your daughter's year concerning threatening and abusive text messages and emails sent by your daughter to her daughter. The messages spell out the consequences if her daughter does not complete a school assignment for your daughter. The girl's parent subsequently sends you copies of the emails and tells you she is considering making a complaint to the police.

You confront your daughter with copies of the emails she sent and explain the impact of the text messages and the email on the girl and the possible legal implications of her actions. Your daughter seems genuinely surprised and remorseful, saying that she did not mean exactly what she had written to the girl.

Action plan

Your teenager incorrectly believes that to maintain her popularity as a leader at school she has to achieve in her school grades. Her unacceptable behaviour may be designed to mask her inability to cope with schoolwork that is becoming increasingly difficult as she progresses through secondary school. She does not realise the impact of her bullying and harassment on the teenager or the potential legal implications of her action.

Seek to work in partnership with the school counsellor to guide and support your daughter to discover and develop her undoubted personal gifts and talents and the personal qualities of dependability, trustworthiness, honesty, humour and reliability and respect for others. Also seek to work in partnership with the school counsellor to reconcile your daughter with the victim and to establish a respectful right relationship with her and other students.

At home ensure the computer is located in clear view in the family room and that the rules for its use include your regular checking of her email. Insist also that when home your daughter's mobile phone is left in a location that allows you to check from time to time the sending and receipt of text messages. Tell your daughter that this will be the rule until you feel she is using her mobile phone in a responsible manner.

Dark thoughts

Your 17-year-old son is in the final year of secondary school. He is a gifted writer and has decided to study journalism after he completes secondary school. One of your son's teachers contacts you with concerns about the dark morbid writing on death and dying they noticed in your son's school notebook. While mildly concerned, you know that your son has a passion for writing poetry and short stories, and pass off the notebook entry as him practising his writing kills. Your son is also in a rock band which disbanded following the death of a band member in a road accident. Shortly after the accident your son gave away his prized guitar and has shown little interest since in the band or music. You become concerned because your son seems to be down on himself most of the time and talks about being useless and being a burden to others. Your concern intensifies when a close friend of your son tells you your son had confided in him that he cannot get over the death of his friend and that he doesn't see any reason to keep on living.

Action plan

In this episode you aren't overly concerned with your son's teacher's comments as you know he has always written about counter-cultural things, and he has been totally immersed in the rock scene. On thinking about it again though, you can see a worrying behaviour pattern. Your son is displaying suicidal tendencies. You should ensure your son experiences unconditional love, that he is listened to, and that he remains connected to the family. Show him trust and try and involve him in decision making in the family. Work through problems with him and give him the message that everyone goes through negative experiences and what is important to focus on is the positives and the gifts he has to share with the world. Finally, do not hesitate to seek professional help for your son if suicidal tendencies persist.

Fair-weather friend

Your daughter has just commenced secondary school. A group of long-time friends from her primary school are also enrolled at the same secondary school. Throughout her primary school years teachers consistently reported your daughter as a caring yet timid girl who loved learning and being with her friends. Your daughter was very much looking forward to secondary school, however, after two days she reported feeling unwell and could not go to school. After four days at home your distraught daughter tells you that she had received a phone call and text message from her closest primary school friend saying that she no longer wanted to continue the friendship. The former friend went on to say that your daughter relied on her too much and that she followed her like a shadow at school, limiting her ability to make new friends.

Action plan

While most teenagers experience a degree of anxiety in the transition from primary to secondary school those with less confidence typically experience great anxiety in the early years of secondary schooling. Your daughter feels abandoned and vulnerable in the new secondary school environment as she believes she no longer has the support of her long-time friend and cannot cope alone.

Your daughter needs reassurance of her fine caring qualities and of the reality that at her present age some teenagers try to increase their popularity in the larger group of students by controlling and manipulating others and by including those they think are popular in their friendship group.

Encourage your daughter to stay connected with her other primary school friends and remind her that her personal qualities become highly regarded in middle and late adolescence. Also seek the advice and support of the school counsellor to build your daughter's self-esteem and to develop and maintain correct respectful relationships with all students in your daughter's friendship group at school.

Family ties

You have been a single parent with one daughter for almost five years. Happily, you have developed what seems to be a promising lasting relationship with your partner who lives some distance away. You sell your small business in the city and move to the coast to be nearer your partner. In so doing you change your 15-year-old daughter's school. You and your partner enjoy a three-week overseas holiday before you move in together in his home. Your mother minds your daughter while you are overseas.

Just before going overseas you learn from your daughter's school that she is misbehaving and not completing homework. It is recommended you undertake an effective parenting program provided by the school but your holiday travel timetable does not allow your participation in the program.

To your dismay, on your return from overseas you learn that your daughter has been extremely rude and misbehaved for both your mother and her school teachers and that she has coloured and cut her hair. Your daughter abuses your partner when he attempts to introduce household rules, saying he is not her father and that she would never do what he said. He angrily replies that she will do as she's told in his house. When you confront your daughter you are also abused. As well, she tells you she wants to live permanently with her father. A similar permanent arrangement when she was 10 lasted for only four weeks. You are very concerned that your partner has told you twice in the last week that your relationship with him won't last if your daughter doesn't comply and recognise him as the head of the household.

Action plan

In this episode you are committing yourself to what appears to be an ongoing relationship. You show your commitment by selling your business, moving house, and changing your daughter's school. Your daughter shows her disapproval with poor behaviour at school and non-acceptance of her mother's partner's attempts to be head of the household.

While it is understandable that you would want your new relationship to work, it is more important for you and your partner to accept the inclusion of your daughter in the relationship — especially as a permanent living arrangement with your daughter's father appears not to be possible. It is also important that your partner accepts you as an equal in the relationship rather than seeing himself as the head of the family. You and your new partner should also participate in a teenager parenting program and seek the support of your daughter's school to address behaviour and school performance issues. Your daughter should also be included in establishing the family view and encouraged and supported in making new friends at school and the wider community.

Greener grass

You are a single mother with a 15-year-old son who has never known his father. You have recently commenced a relationship with a same-sex partner who now lives with you. This is your second same-sex partner and you are very happy in the relationship. You have always experienced difficulty managing your son's challenging behaviour which in recent times has escalated to him wilfully destroying property. He openly tells you and your partner of his opposition to people of the same sex being together saying that it causes him great embarrassment with his male football friends. While your son portrays an image of a tough rugged outdoor male he also has a gentle caring side being genuinely supportive of the disadvantaged in the community. Your son recognises that he has difficulty managing his behaviour and has sought assistance from the student counsellor at his school. He also sought advice from the student counsellor on the education standard required to join the defence forces.

You reach a point where you believe he can no longer live at home and you relocate him to live with his aunt some 100 km away. Your son enrols at the local secondary school but it is not long before he calls and pleads with you to re-enrol him at his former secondary school. You refuse, saying he did not deserve to be given another chance at his former school. Your son subsequently contacts his former school and is told that he would, with his mother's permission, be accepted back in his former school community. Your son finds a family living 25 minutes from his former school who are prepared to have him live with them so he can attend his initial secondary school. The counsellor from his present secondary school contacts you telling you that your son was very unhappy at his new school and is likely to drop out of school. The counsellor recommends that your son lives with the family offering accommodation within travelling distance to his former school and home.

Action plan

Given your preferred lifestyle and your son's adamant opposition it is unlikely you could all live together in a happy relationship at this time. Yet your son seems genuinely unhappy at his present school and has gone to great lengths to secure accommodation that will enable him to return to his original school. He also appears to have established a sound, potentially productive relationship with the school counsellor, is prepared to address his anger management issues and has a clear career goal.

It is more likely that you will develop and maintain an ongoing positive relationship with your son if you support his wish to live away from, yet near you, and to attend his original secondary school. Make contact with the school counsellor and work in partnership to support your son to achieve his career goal and independence.

It would also be helpful to contact your son's football coach with a view to gaining an appropriate male mentor/life coach who could help your son.

Hidden gift

You are experiencing increasing difficulty in engaging your 14-year-old son with the family, school and the broader community. During primary school a specialist assessment diagnosed him to be of above average intelligence with a specific learning disability. As a consequence, he received additional support for reading and writing. He maintained an interest in learning and developed a keen interest in fish breeding as a hobby. He often amazed visiting family and friends with his vast and detailed knowledge of fish breeding.

In recent times he has disengaged with learning at school. His challenging behaviour at school has seen him spend significant time out of the classroom and suspended from school. At home he has become increasingly self-critical and distant from other members of the family.

Action plan

Your son needs to build his self-esteem and reconnect with life. Remind him of his superior knowledge of fish breeding and encourage him to excel as a fish breeder and to see fish breeding as a possible career opportunity.

Support your son in connecting with others interested in this niche area and in developing the personal qualities of responsibility, trustworthiness, dependability, honesty and a sense of humour that will enhance his success in business. Look for support from your son's school in selecting subjects that best accommodate his learning disability and in gaining school-based work experience in a field related to his area of interest.

Hot breakfast

You are having breakfast with your two sons. The eldest is sitting in a certain chair preferred by both boys. When your eldest son leaves the room for a brief period your youngest son immediately sits in the preferred chair knowing that his brother had been sitting there. On returning to the kitchen the older brother demands that the younger brother move off the chair. The younger brother refuses, claiming that the older brother had moved. The older brother begins to use force to move the younger brother who protests that he is being hurt and that the older brother did the same thing to him yesterday. You tell the older boy not to hurt his brother. He says he doesn't care and keeps hitting and pushing him, getting more physical by the minute. You keep telling the older brother to sit down. He eventually sits in another chair after verbally abusing his younger brother.

Action plan

In this episode the younger brother is seeking attention. He is also challenging for power over his older, physically stronger brother. The older brother retaliates using force and verbal abuse to maintain his position in the family. A way forward here is to agree to include in the family view the rule that there is no reserved seating in the house. If you leave it you lose it. The effects of the brother's behaviour in disrupting the family enjoying breakfast together should also be discussed, with an emphasis placed on the importance of respectful relationships between members of the family.

Hung up

You and your daughter have been waiting to use the home phone for some time. It becomes free and you both rush to use it. You accidentally pinch your daughter's arm as you wrestle for the phone. Your daughter reacts by throwing the phone to the floor and slapping you on the face. She also verbally abuses you and slams every door on the way to her bedroom. You follow her angrily telling her never to slap you again and that she will have to pay to replace the phone.

Action plan

In this situation it would have been better for the effective functioning of the family had you not been drawn into an angry exchange of words and had given yourself and your daughter time and space to cool down. The issue should, however, be discussed and not left unresolved. Not reacting to your daughter's angry outburst would have been very difficult to do; a better course of action would have been to discuss the rules of the family view and, in particular, the rules that everyone in the family deserves and should give respect to each other. Try and establish a rule of using the home phone that accommodates everyone's needs in the family, and also don't be afraid to give or accept an apology for actions not really intended. Always ensure your daughter knows she is loved unconditionally and belongs in the family.

Hurt

You are divorced with a 13-year-old daughter who is attending a small co-education secondary school. Your daughter attended a rural primary school where she excelled academically and represented the region in athletics and swimming. When she commenced secondary school she achieved As and Bs in her end-of-year report card, with positive comments about her academic and sporting abilities and her potential as a future school leader.

Her father has remarried and lives overseas with his second wife and several children. Since returning home from spending the summer school vacation with her father and his new family, your daughter's attitude and behaviour at home and at school has deteriorated rapidly.

At home she is often moody, frequently uses foul language and shows you little to no respect. You were recently contacted by her school, concerned that her performance in all subjects had fallen dramatically and that her challenging behaviour resulted in her having to spend ever-increasing time in lunchtime detention.

Action plan

Your daughter's visit to her father appears to have been the catalyst for her uncharacteristic behaviour towards you and her lack of interest, application and poor performance at school.

While continuing to parent with purpose, maintain focus on achieving the parent wish you have for your teenager. Be prepared at this time to overlook small indiscretions and look for and reinforce any effort she makes to commit herself again to be the very best she can be in her life.

It would also be useful to identify an adult in her life that she admires and to enlist their support to become her mentor. Such a person can, over time, help rebuild her self-esteem and desire to apply herself to be the best she can be in her life.

Money matters

A long-time friend of your 13-year-old daughter is having a birthday party. You give your daughter $50 over and above her weekly allowance to buy her friend a birthday card and gift. To your dismay your daughter returns from shopping, not with a birthday card and a gift for her friend, but a new pair of jeans. On questioning your daughter, she says the jeans were the latest style of her favourite designer label, and were at a once-only discounted bargain price. She also tells you she borrowed $30 from another friend to purchase the jeans.

Action plan

Your daughter is showing immature, irresponsible behaviour. Discuss with your daughter in a calm manner your disappointment in her actions, which showed no respect for the trust you had placed in her or for the financial impact her reckless spending would have on the functioning of the family. Again, in a calm yet definite manner, tell your daughter that she will have to go without her regular financial allowance until the amount is repaid. In so doing, reassure her that while you didn't like nor can accept her action, she remains a loved member of the family and can regain your trust through her actions.

On the edge

You have recently remarried. You have two teenagers, a 16-year-old boy and a 13-year-old girl. The children have irregular contact with their father and seem to have a fair relationship with their stepfather who shows genuine interest in their wellbeing. You are taking anti-depressant medication and believe you are too soft in your parenting, of your son in particular.

You are becoming increasingly concerned about your son's defiant, manipulative and challenging behaviour at home, as well as the group of friends with whom he is spending significant time. Recently, your son's school contacted you about his lack of application in all subjects and his frequent absences from school. Comments in school reports have been that he has the ability but does not apply himself. Your son is physically strong for his age, showing above average ability and great potential in most sporting activities. He currently lives with his father through the week and spends some weekends with you. He has mentioned in passing that he would like to join the defence force. Over the past month your son has been warned twice by police in relation to his involvement with a group of youths using and selling illicit drugs. His father, on learning of his behaviour and lack of application at school, told him he was useless and destined for jail.

Action plan

Your son is at high risk of progressively disengaging with school, furthering his involvement with a problematic group of youths, and finding himself entering the juvenile justice system with little hope of achieving his full potential in life.

You need to urgently establish and maintain partnerships with significant people in your son's life-world to develop and implement a support plan. Significant people include you, his father, an adult he respects and/or the school guidance counsellor/student wellbeing officer.

The first step is to provide stability and predictability in his life by deciding where best it is for him to live. Given your health and ability to manage his behaviour it would be best for him to live with his father and to maintain regular scheduled time with you. Agree on and maintain a parenting strategy that rewards responsible behaviour with an appropriate amount of independence. Remember, you are the leader of your family just as his father is the leader of his family. It is essential that both parents show and maintain their respective leadership role as parents.

Encourage your son to make use of his physical ability by joining a sporting association or related organisation and in so doing meet people of his age who make right choices for themselves and care about their personal wellbeing. Assist him to establish and maintain a clear career goal by helping him identify the entry requirements for the defence force and related careers. Seek the support of his school to encourage him to complete school and to ensure he undertakes the required course of study to ensure his eligibility for his preferred career. Finally, encourage and where possible, assist him to secure part-time paid employment to provide an income and regular daily routine.

Off the rails

You have three children, two boys aged 19 and 17, and a 15-year-old daughter. You work part-time outside of the home and your husband works long hours in a job that requires him to be often away from home for several days at a time. Your eldest son is a university student and your other son is in his first year as an apprentice tradesman. Your daughter has performed well above average throughout her primary school years and her first two years at secondary school. She is a capable athlete, has many friends and finds it easy to find part-time work. She is heavily influenced by the media and spends almost all she earns on new clothes. Her greatest joy is to spend time with her friends at the local shopping mall. This year she is showing little interest in her schoolwork and her grades have dropped from As to Cs in all subjects.

Recently you were shocked and disappointed to learn from a friend that she saw your daughter at the local shopping mall with a boy. The boy was known in the neighbourhood for his use of illicit drugs. This was particularly worrying as earlier that day you had dropped her off at her part-time job. On checking with her employer you are told that she left soon after arriving, saying she was feeling ill and wanted to go home. Just yesterday you received a call from her school reporting that she had truanted school and was seen with a group of teenagers in the local shopping mall.

Action plan

It is essential that you and your husband work together and use the same approach to your daughter's behaviour. Resist overreacting to her deceit, her possible involvement in drugs and her falling grades at school. Your daughter knows right from wrong and is a student of above average ability. See her as going temporarily off the rails. It would be useful to gain the involvement of a relevant person — perhaps her school counsellor — to mediate a meeting involving you, your husband and your daughter. In the meeting remind your daughter that while you will always love her you do not accept her present behaviour. Remind her of the safety implications of not knowing where she was and the health risk associated with being involved with drugs.

Make it clear that she will have to act responsibly for some time to regain your trust. Work in partnership with her school to monitor her progress and set clear rules on how and when she is to communicate with you when she is away from homes. Finally, be prepared to review the rules of communication when your daughter consistently behave appropriately and praise her for any improved performance at school.

Runaway

Both of your daughters are in secondary school. Your 15-year-old is in her second last year and the 12-year-old is in the first year of her secondary school. Her teachers believe your eldest daughter has the potential to be a high achiever but are very concerned that she is not performing to her ability. Your daughter's primary school reports suggest that she excelled in all areas and was a committed popular student.

While her performance in her first years of secondary school was *Very good* to *Excellent* in all subject areas, her performance fell significantly in the second half of her third year in secondary school. The number of days absent and/or late also doubled in the second half of her third year. During her third year your daughter became the girlfriend of a low-achieving boy who was expelled from her school for ongoing challenging behaviour. The boy was an above average footballer who enjoyed popularity with some students for his sporting ability. Your daughter regards herself as unattractive and lost most of her friends over her blind devotion to a boy whose antisocial behaviour had attracted the attention of the police on more than one occasion. You try without success to counsel your daughter to discontinue the relationship and ground her for lying about seeing him after school. You also try to curb her use of the home phone and email to keep in constant contact with the boy. During a heated argument over the relationship your daughter leaves home. She was subsequently returned home by the police after spending the night with the boy in a local park.

Action plan

Your daughter feels she is not attractive and is determined to keep her first boyfriend. She's blind to the advice of her friends about the boy, is not applying herself to her schoolwork and is staying away from school to be with him. Show your daughter your trust and respect her right to choose her boyfriend. Agree that she can see him every day as long as she is home by dark and that she can either make one phone call or spend 15 minutes emailing him daily as long as she attends school and makes satisfactory progress with her schoolwork. Your goal is for your potentially bright daughter not to drop out of school but to complete her secondary schooling to give her the option in the future of pursuing a tertiary education. Seek the support of your daughter's school for the provision of any needed catch-up tuition and/or personal counselling, and ensure your daughter has medical advice on issues related to the practice of safe sex.

Scratcher

Recently you received communication from your 14-year-old son's school that he was behaving unacceptably and had not completed homework assignments. His primary school report cards had previously consistently described him as a likeable, mischievous child who showed little interest in schoolwork. There was a remark by one primary school teacher that suggested your son may have a learning disability but this was never fully investigated.

Your son was also regarded as a gifted footballer and enjoyed great popularity with his peers. With the exception of this year your son had been selected in the regional representative football team. His failure to make this years' representative football team greatly upset your son. You notice that none of his friends come around to your home anymore and the once sound sleeper is now a restless sleeper. You also notice a number of scratches on his hands and legs. You ask him about the scratches and he volunteers that scratching himself made him feel better.

Action plan

Your son is experiencing a great deal of uncertainty and unhappiness in his life at this time. His self-esteem is low. He has always enjoyed great popularity with his sporting ability and outgoing likeable larrikin nature. His non-selection in the regional representative football team has, however, brought him to question himself about his ability and worth in life. His unacceptable behaviour at school could be in part in response to him experiencing a learning disability which was evident in his primary school years. The learning disability would be increasingly difficult to conceal as secondary school work becomes more demanding. It is important at this time to reassure your son of his worth. Seek support from his school to cater for his learning disability to ensure he is engaged in the most appropriate course of study. It would also be useful to seek out a mentor or trusted guide for your son for his sport. A talented athlete does not cease to be talented, and with guidance he could regain representative football selection and continue a sporting career. His potential in other fields should be investigated and encouraged. Above all, he should always feel he is a respected member of the family who is loved and valued for who he is.

Spellbound

You and your husband have been happily married for 27 years. You have two adult sons and a much-loved 16-year-old daughter. You maintain regular contact with your relations and your family is highly regarded in the community. Your daughter works regularly as a volunteer in a local community organisation. Everyone she meets see her as a warm, caring, kind-hearted girl. Up until this year she has been a consistent high achiever at school.

Recently you were contacted by her school, concerned over her frequent absences and dramatic decline in achievement in all subjects. Over the last summer school vacation your daughter's relationship with the 26-year-old brother of your daughter-in-law, whom she had known for almost 10 years as a relation, became tense and intimate.

You and your husband are devastated, especially in learning that this man has a history of forming relationships with 16-year-old girls, and that he has a criminal history, is a drug user and is unemployed. While you and your husband, your sons and your relations counsel your daughter against continuing the relationship she is spellbound and believes everything he says. Just recently your daughter tells you she is dropping out of school as he has told her she doesn't need to finish school.

Action plan

The circumstance your daughter is currently in is understandably of great concern. Your sound advice is falling on deaf ears. What is needed is for you and your husband to keep the lifelong parent wish you have for your daughter in mind and not to blame yourself or remain fixed on her present action. Your daughter needs to know that while you will always love her and be there for her you do not agree with the choices she is presently making. While ensuring key family are maintained, be prepared to live with the current circumstance in the short term. Ensure her physical wellbeing and seek the support of her school to relax school assignment requirements to keep her connected with her peers. Try to establish if there is a young women, perhaps a favourite teacher, who she admires and trusts. Seek her help as a mentor or life coach for your daughter to be her friend and confidant. Hopefully over time this relationship will build her self-respect and eventually expose the 26-year-old for who he really is and what he is doing to prevent your daughter from realising her potential in life.

Self-exile

You have two teenage children. An outgoing, bright, 17-year-old boy and a sensitive, timid, 13-year-old daughter. You recently withdrew your daughter from a large co-educational secondary school as she was the brunt of bullying. You enrolled her in a small co-educational school and sought assistance from the school to help her make a fresh start. While the school has been very supportive in trying to include your daughter they have reported to you that she is choosing to isolate herself from her peers. Your daughter's developmental history is that she achieved milestones late and that she was a clumsy, poorly coordinated child. Her primary school teachers consistently reported that she had poor social skills and also that she struggled with mathematics but that she displayed potential in art and written expression.

Every day for the past week your daughter has phoned you from school saying she was being ignored by everyone and that she wanted you to collect her and take her home. For the past six weeks your daughter has been attending weekly counselling sessions with a doctor and is currently taking prescribed anti-depression medication.

Action plan

Your daughter's developmental history makes it likely she will experience difficulty mastering the typical teenager developmental tasks related to social competence. As well it is highly likely that she will experience difficulty achieving academically at secondary school, particularly in mathematics. She may therefore feel inadequate and even resentful that her brother has confidence and succeeds while she finds it hard to make and keep friends and achieve high marks at school.

Your aim should be to develop and maintain partnerships with and between you and your daughter's school counsellor or pastoral care teacher, her teachers and her therapist, to consider her needs and to develop a support action plan to be adopted by all in her lifeworld. The support action plan should aim at developing and maintaining her overall resilience and, in particular, her self-esteem and social skills. Your daughter needs to feel and experience that she can succeed socially. At school, her social skills could be developed by assigning her a buddy and by including her in structured group activities. As well, the school should ensure she receives appropriate assistance with mathematics. Your daughter's self-esteem could also be developed by encouraging her to develop her identified potential in art and written expression, both in school and through joining art and or writing clubs outside of school.

Newcomer

A work transfer has meant that you had to relocate your family interstate. Your 14-year-old outgoing, gregarious daughter protests loudly about leaving all her friends but reluctantly accepts that the family has no choice but to move.

You enrol your daughter in a small coeducational school close to your new address. Within a fortnight you receive a phone call from the school counsellor concerned about how your daughter is settling into her new school. You are told that your daughter has been distraught a number of times over being excluded by her peers. You are also told that a number of students in your daughter's year level had reported concerns over things your daughter told them she had done in the past, including being sexually promiscuous and drinking alcohol. Your daughter's peers felt that while she had likeable qualities and could easily be accepted by the group, her outrageous stories were risking her being excluded from her peer group.

Action plan

Your daughter's likeable qualities have already been recognised by her peers. The key is for your daughter to realise that it would be difficult for any teenager her age to gain immediate acceptance as friendship groups would be well established in her new school. Your daughter needs to be patient and have confidence in her known personal qualities and not continue putting around untrue stories to sensationalise herself. It would also be helpful for you to work in partnership with the school counsellor to monitor your daughter's progress and to provide encouragement as she establishes herself in her new school.

Over-indulged

You have been living as a single parent for the past 10 years. You work in a remote location and have recently renewed contact after six years with your 13-year-old son who lives interstate with his grandparents. His mother has remarried and lives near the grandparents. Your son is in his first year of high school. His grandparents tell you the school is concerned that he is experiencing great anxiety at school — often crying and needing to contact his grandparents through the day for reassurance. This behaviour was not apparent during your son's primary school years. It appears that the grandparents are responding to your son's every whim — buying him the latest designer clothing, expensive sportswear, personal computer, games console and mobile phone.

You spend an enjoyable holiday with your son and are keen to have an ongoing presence in his life. You, your son and his grandparents are unsure if it would be best for the teenager to live with you or remain living with his grandparents near his mother in a school renowned for providing a caring friendly safe learning environment.

Action plan

The extreme anxiety displayed by your son could stem from the combined effect of mild anxiety experienced by most teenagers on commencing high school with your re-entry to his life after six years. Even though your son is being over-indulged by his doting grandparents, the nature and location of the high school provides him with a high-quality, safe learning environment.

While reuniting with your son and wanting to maintain the relationship offers great potential in life for you both, continuing to live with his grandparents and attending the highly regarded school is preferred over coming to live with you in a remote location. The relationship between you and your son can grow and remain strong by establishing and maintaining regular contact with each other. Both of you could agree to contact each other by phone or text message once per week and spend time together every school holidays. It could also be agreed that his enrolment at the school could be reviewed at the end of the semester. The grandparents could also help themselves and the teenager by undertaking a teenager parenting program to learn about today's teenagers and how to effectively parent to ensure the teenager achieves their full potential in life.

Independence

You have a blended family with an opinionated 16-year-old daughter and 17-year-old stepson in his final year of high school. While you have a loving relationship with your partner it is also volatile, with frequent heated arguments and time spent apart. Your daughter is strong-willed and argumentative and often clashes with members of the family, in particular her stepbrother. Typically, your home is a noisy place.

Recently your daughter and her friend and your stepson were home alone. Even though your daughter and her friend knew your stepson was studying they played loud music and constantly interrupted his studying. After repeatedly having his request for quiet ignored your stepson swore loudly broke a vase and damaged the bedroom door as he quickly packed some of his clothes and angrily left the house, saying he had had enough and would not be living there anymore.

A week later you received a telephone call from your stepson's school concerned that he had been staying with a different student each night since he left home and that his performance in his all-important final year at school had fallen sharply particularly in the past week.

Action plan

While your home has never been a quiet place, your son has been able to cope and complete his schoolwork. However, in his final year of high school he needs to have the best possible study conditions at home to maximise his school results and give himself more options in the future.

The family, in particular the daughter, need to work together in right relationships and give special consideration to a family member at an important time of the life. Any student needs to be living in a stable predictable environment to achieve their best possible result in the final year of high school. Any thoughts of your son continuing to 'couch surf' at a school friend's home should not be entertained. The plans of your stepson to live independently should be held off until school is completed.

Real friend

You have a fun-loving teenage daughter who looks forward to spending as much time as possible with her friends. She has always been popular with children her age and has quickly established herself in a new friendship group soon after going to high school. Friends are at the centre of your teenager's life. Not only does she spend time with their friends every day at school she seems to be in constant communication with them before and after school.

Every day in the past week your daughter has arrived home from school upset. After several days she tells you that the most popular person in the friendship group was encouraging others in the group to exclude your daughter from the group. This was because she had been spending time with a teenager who had been excluded from the group for sending threatening text messages to a member of the group. The excluded member was the only member of the group who had previously supported your teenager following the death of a much-loved relative.

Action plan

Your teenager should be commended for the loyalty and friendship she has given to the friend who had supported her during a difficult personal time. Your teenager should be encouraged to tell her friends why she was supporting the teenager. It is likely members of the group will understand and admire your teenager for being a loyal friend. Authentic friendship and loyalty is an attribute highly regarded by teenagers. As your teenager has the personal qualities that have always been popular with her peers it is likely the group of friends will accept her continuing to spend time with the excluded teenager while retaining membership in the group. Your teenager could also use her standing in the group to help reconcile the excluded teenager with the group.

Schemer

You have a 15-year-old daughter who has performed above average in her first two years of high school. This year however, friendships have been the only thing of importance to your daughter. Two teenagers your daughter have been mixing with recently left saying the school was too strict.

Since the two girls left your daughter has been constantly critical of the school saying that teachers were picking on her, that she had no friends and that the teaching and range of subjects at the school were below standard. Your daughter promises you she will apply herself to her schoolwork if you allow her to enrol at the same school as her two friends.

Action plan

Your daughter is scheming to gain your approval to join her two friends at their new school. It is unlikely that changing schools will improve your daughter's application to her schoolwork or her behaviour as both friends are underachieving disruptive students. What is likely is that you will only be transferring the problem to another place.

You need to make it clear to your daughter that you will not consider changing schools while her results and behaviour are poor. Agree to review her enrolment at her present school in six months if she performs to her ability and behaves appropriately at school.

Chapter

7

In conclusion

As we have seen in the preceding pages, parenting a teenager is a journey of discovery for both the parent and the teenager. For some, that journey can be very difficult. A teenager who experiences ongoing family dysfunction, or who has a significant learning disability, severe challenging behaviour, or substance misuse will frequently experience difficulty mastering the developmental tasks associated with normal adolescent development. It is in these extreme cases that parenting purposefully and with patience will give the best chance for both parent and teenager to survive the journey with healthy self-esteem and a productive future.

But even if your experience so far as a parent has been relatively 'normal' (whatever that is these days) the teen scenarios we have just covered show how important it is to never give up on your teenager. Keeping focused on your Parent Wish and using your Touchstone in trying times will help to ground you and keep your role of parent firmly in your sights.

It is often tempting to feel that you must connect with your teenager on their terms as you feel increasingly isolated from their teenage culture and seek to avoid being labelled 'old' and 'out of touch'. But you cannot ultimately communicate with them as their own friends would. That is not your role and it is not how they see you. They may resent being controlled by a parent and lash out at you but if you try to be anything but their parent you leave them without an essential role model at a vital time in their lives.

That's not to say that a parent is always someone who has to interact with their teenager in a dominating role. Being friendly, polite and respectful are healthy ways for both teenagers and adults to communicate with each other. Communication helps keep people connected. Teenagers should stay connected to parents, their family, their school, and their sporting or specific interest groups in the community. The outcome for a teenager who finds themselves disconnected prematurely can be quite bleak. Leaving school early can bring about a future of part-time unskilled work, long periods of unemployment, poor physical and mental health, and an increased chance of entering the juvenile justice system, with little likelihood of ever achieving their full potential in life.

Ultimately, on this journey through the teenage years the best outcome for both parent and teenager rests with your commitment to learning who you and your teenager really are. Everyone has different gifts and it does not matter what those gifts might be or how unconventional they may seem. What matters is that they are regarded as being of worth. Our role as parents is to discover and nurture your teenager's gifts and build self-value in our teenager by adding vital personal skills, including the community-valued qualities of responsibility, trustworthiness, honesty, commitment, reliability and a sense of humour.